Colors: Blue

Esther Sarfatti

Rourke
Publishing LLC
Vero Beach, Florida 32964

www.rourkepublishing.com

PHOTO CREDITS: © Marilyn Nieves: title page; © Viorika Prikhodko: page 3; © Nicole Young: page 5; © Olga Lyubkina: page 7; © Nathan Wood: page 9; © Anna Sirotina: page 11; © James Blinn: page 13; © Tony Sanchez-Espinosa: page 15; © Frank Leung: page 17; © Devon Stephens: page 21; © Nick Stubbs, © Irene Teesalu, © Troy E. Parker: page 23.

Editor: Robert Stengard-Olliges

Cover design by Nicola Stratford, bdpublishing.com

Library of Congress Cataloging-in-Publication Data

Sarfatti, Esther.
  Colors : blue / Esther Sarfatti.
      p. cm. -- (Concepts)
  ISBN 978-1-60044-517-0 (Hardcover)
  ISBN 978-1-60044-658-0 (Softcover)
  1. Colors--Juvenile literature. 2. Blue--Juvenile literature. I. Title.
  QC495.5.S355 2008
  535.6--dc22
                            2007012300

Rourke Publishing
Printed in the United States of America, North Mankato, Minnesota
081810
081710LP-A

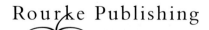

Rourke Publishing

www.rourkepublishing.com – rourke@rourkepublishing.com
Post Office Box 3328, Vero Beach, FL 32964

This page is blue.

Blue is my favorite color.

I like blueberries.

I like blue eyes.

I like blue butterflies.

I like blue wheels.

I like blue kites.

I like blue birds.

17

I like the blue sky.

19

I like the blue water.

So many things are blue.
Do you like blue, too?

Index

Further Reading

Anderson, Moira. *Finding Colors: Blue*. Heinemann, 2005.
Schuette, Sarah L. *Blue: Seeing Blue All Around Us*.
  Capstone Press, 2006.

Recommended Websites

www.enchantedlearning.com/colors/blue.shtml

About the Author

Esther Sarfatti has worked with children's books for over 15 years as an editor and translator. This is her first series as an author. Born in Brooklyn, New York, and brought up in a trilingual home, Esther currently lives with her husband and son in Madrid, Spain.